miami

AND SOUTH BEACH

a photographic portrait

First published in the United States
of America by:

Twin Lights Publishers, Inc.
10 Hale Street
Rockport, Massachusetts 01966
Telephone: (978) 546-7398
http://www.twinlightspub.com

and

PilotPress Publishers, Inc.
110 Weschester Road
Newton, Massachusetts 02458
Telephone: (617) 335-0703
http://www.PilotPress.com

ISBN 1-885435-29-0

10 9 8 7 6 5 4 3 2 1

Book design by
SYP Design & Production, Inc.
http://www.sypdesign.com

Cover Photo by: Louis Novick
Back Cover Photos by: Goran Matijasevic
and Carol Verneuil

Printed in China

Other titles in the
Photographic Portrait series:

Cape Ann
Kittery to the Kennebunks
The Mystic Coast, Stonington to New London
The White Mountains
Boston's South Shore
Upper Cape Cod
The Rhode Island Coast
Naples, Florida
Portland, Maine
Mid and Lower Cape Cod
The Berkshires
Camden, Maine

contents

ACKNOWLEDGEMENT

Twin Lights Publishers and PilotPress Publishers wish to thank all of the photographers who submitted their work for our consideration. Because of space limitations, we were unable to include many excellent photographs in *Miami and South Beach Florida: a Photographic Portrait*. Miami and South Beach are a fertile area for many talented resident professional and amateur photographers. The natural beauty attracts visitors to record its special qualities at all times of the year.

Special thanks go to Abbi Goodman and Peter McGee who organized and supervised the photography contest. Their efficiency and thoroughness made the judging of over 1,000 entries a less difficult task.

We extend our gratitude to the judges of the Miami and South Beach Florida Regional Photography Contest., Nancy Moore and Steve Dorfman. Nancy Moore is the publisher and editor in chief of the regional city magazine, *Miami Metro*, as well as the publisher of several other custom publications produced by Florida Media Affiliates. She has been at the helm of *Miami Metro* since its 1998 inception, and oversaw its transformation from what was formerly known as *South Florida Magazine*.

Steve Dorfman is the managing editor of the regional city magazine, *Miami Metro*, and several other custom publications produced by Florida Media Affiliates.

He has been with *Miami Metro* since 1999. During his tenure, the magazine has won nearly two dozen editorial and design awards from the Florida Magazine Association and the Society of Professional Journalists. We are pleased with their selections and are indebted to them.

Lauri Garbo, who wrote the major part of the Miami section, contributes regularly to *Florida Gulf Coast* lifestyle magazines and newspapers. She obtained a B.A. in English from Adolphus College and a M. Ed. from the University of South Florida. Garbo's company, Write For You!, also provides writing services for public relations firms, advertising agencies, and corporations.

Sarah FK Coble is a nationally published freelance writer. She is also a contributor to *Florida International Magazine*, *Naples Illustrated*, and the *Naples Literary Review*. Her work has been published in the *Sanibel Captiva Review*, *Gulfshore Life*, *Gulfshore Style* and *Home and Condo* magazines. Sarah FK Coble wrote the South Beach section and additional captions for the Miami section.

In writing the captions, they have found evocative titles and added facts to bring out the history and local color for each photograph. We think they have given an added dimension to the book.

Finally, our thanks go to designer Sara Day who has created a beautiful book.

miami

early Seminole and Micco-sukee Indian tribes, famed Spanish explorers, and Flagler's powerful steam locomotive all contributed to Miami's formation.

A four-mile coastal ridge served as Miami's initial settlement in the first decade of the 20th century. An enterprising engineering plan to drain the Everglades changed the topography of Miami forever from a swampy wetland to the sophisticated international metropolis that exists today. Images found on these pages provide a glimpse into Miami's past and a collage of lifestyles that compose Miami's unique culture today.

Photographs of the historic Biltmore Hotel, the grand Vizcaya estate, and renovated Art Deco hotels along South Beach illustrate the prestige and glamour upheld by Miami's most affluent residents and guests. Retail destinations like Bayside Marketplace and CocoWalk combined with skyscrapers of downtown Miami and towering luxury condominiums cater to the whims and desires of upscale clientele. Ethic enclaves such as Little Haiti and Little Havana retain the cultural heritage of those seeking a better way of life. All of these images illustrate a contemporary Miami with its cultural contrasts and commercial influence.

The natural side of Miami has maintained its presence, adorning coastlines and barrier islands and stretching far into the Everglades. Graceful egrets and imposing alligators are reminders of the natural beauty that once dominated the area.

The vibrant spirit of Miami has emerged from ravaging hurricanes, cultural diversity, and courageous entrepreneurs. Each image in this photographic record reveals one small piece of the complex and unique metropolis called Miami.

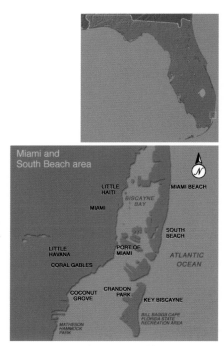

Miami and South Beach area

LITTLE HAITI — BISCAYNE BAY — MIAMI BEACH — MIAMI — SOUTH BEACH — LITTLE HAVANA — PORT OF MIAMI — ATLANTIC OCEAN — CORAL GABLES — COCONUT GROVE — CRANDON PARK — KEY BISCAYNE — BILL BAGGS CAPE FLORIDA STATE RECREATION AREA — MATHESON HAMMOCK PARK

FIRST PLACE

Trades and Tides

LOUIS NOVICK
NIKON F3

The Miami River upholds its tradition of flowing commerce as the fifth largest port in the state of Florida.

Louis Novick has been a Miami resident for over 15 years, and the award-winning photographs in this collection reveal his love for and understanding of the area. His ability to capture the magic in everyday scenes reveals his artistry and unique perspective.

His broad experience in photography spans over three decades. He has photographed Hollywood's most notable celebrities, national political figures, and Fortune 500 CEO's.

Currently he owns and operates an independent photographic studio and works with advertising agencies and art directors who handle prestigious clients including, Cartier, Saks, and Sony. In addition, his work frequently appears on the cover of *Selecta*, an international society and fashion magazine.

Mr. Novick attended the Maryland Institute College of Art and has broad photographic experience, ranging from management and studio photography to freelance work. His on-line portfolio may be accessed at www.lounovick.com.

SECOND PLACE

Hues at Nightfall

LOUIS NOVICK
NIKON F3

An explosion of color ushers in
Miami's nightlife from chic Collins
Avenue to the tourist haven of
Bayside Marketplace.

THIRD PLACE

Poised

LOUIS NOVICK
NIKON F3
EPY

Amidst a dense concentration of office buildings in downtown Miami, International Place makes a patriotic statement. This 48-story building was designed by internationally renowned architect I.M. Pei.

downtown
AND NORTH

(above)

**Miami Juxtapositions:
High Rise Art, Used Cars**

COURTESY OF
GORAN MATIJASEVIC
MINOLTA XE-7
FUJICHROME 100

Every street in Miami offers a unique
perspective of Miami's unique artistic, architectural and cultural mix.

(right)

Punching Out

LOUIS NOVICK
NIKON F3

Silhouettes of towering office buildings and prestigious condominiums
are passionately enveloped in a South
Florida sunset.

(above)

New Day

LOUIS NOVICK
NIKON F3

Tranquil waters usher in a new day to Miami's shores where international business begins long before dawn.

(left)

Afternoon Shadows

ERNEST PICK
NIKON F4
VELVIA

Architectural influences from Spain highlight the exterior window on the Aqua Vista residence. Mediterranean styles dominate the design style of both residential and commercial structures.

Praise

ERNEST PICK
FUJI, MEDIUM FORMAT
VELVIA, F-16

Swaying palms, a symbol of South Florida, seem to reach toward the warm Florida Sun. A dry winter climate and blue sky welcome winter tourists.

(above)

Cruise Capital

LOUIS NOVICK
NIKON F3

Regularly scheduled lifeboat drills
reveal the practical side of luxurious
cruising from the Port of Miami. In
fiscal year 2000, more that 3.3 million
passengers used the port.

(opposite)

Freedom Soars

LAURIE BARKER COE
NIKON N90 S

Built in 1925 and restored in 1988,
this Spanish baroque building originally served the *Miami Daily News*.
Cubans fleeing Castro in the 1960's
sought the Freedom Tower as the
Cuban Refugee Center.

(above)

City Meets Sea

JUDY CASELEY

The mouth of the Miami River spills into Biscayne Bay just south of Bayfront Park.

(left)

Eternal Flame

HEATHER J. KIRK
OLYMPUS IS-10 SUPER DELUXE
KODAK-64 EKTACHROME

Located in the Little Havana section of Miami, the memorial honors the martyrs of the Assault Brigade to Cuba, which became the Bay of Pigs incident.

(opposite)

Spaniard Salute

JUDY CASELEY
NIKON F4
KODAK 200, F-8

After discovering the east coast of Florida near St. Augustine, Ponce de Leon sailed south to Biscayne Bay. He referred to the Miami area as "Tequesta." His voyage is commemorated with this monument located near Bayside.

JUAN PONCE DE LEON

HE ARRIVED ON EASTER SUNDAY
IN 1513 LOOKING FOR THE
FOUNTAIN OF YOUTH. HE
FOUND SOMETHING BETTER,
A BEAUTIFUL LAND THAT HE
CLAIMED FOR SPAIN, AND HE
CALLED IT FLORIDA.

Donated by the Government of Spain in 1976
Re-dedicated on May 22, 1995

Illuminating Tiers

LOUIS NOVICK
NIKON F3
KPY

Encircled with light, International
Place serves as Miami's commercial
landmark. This skyscraper uses colored lighting to reflect seasonal
changes and holidays.

City Tour

COURTESY OF
GORAN MATIJASEVIC
MINOLTA XE-7
FUJICHROME 100

Horses and carriages offer an old
fashioned, romantic way to view
Miami's sleek, modern skyline.

Neon Magic

DAVID L. JONES
CANNON EOSI
35MM, F-8 ° SEC.

Parades and festival abound in
Miami, providing a variety of ethnic
experiences year round.

Nationsbank Tower by Night

COURTESY OF
GORAN MATIJASEVIC
MINOLTA XE-7
FUJICHROME 100

Built in 1983 during the banking
boom of that decade, and originally
known as CenTrust Tower, the
Nationsbank Tower is the Miami's
skyline's most striking feature.

(left)

Looking Deep

LOUIS NOVICK
NIKON F3

Legendary coach Don Shula and quarterback Dan Marino led the Miami Dolphins to national fame. Fans continue to flood Pro Player Stadium for some of the NFL's greatest games.

(below)

Hike!

LOUIS NOVICK
NIKON F3

Quarterback Dan Marino of the Miami Dolphins ignites the crowd at Pro Player Stadium.

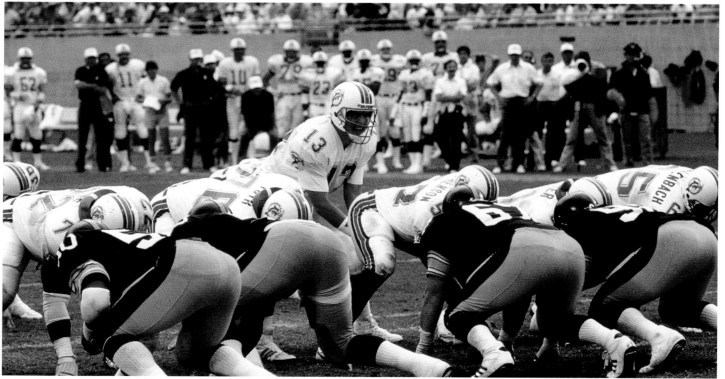

Prep

LOUIS NOVICK
NIKON F3
E100S

Pro Player Stadium receives final preparations for Super Bowl XXXIII when the Denver Broncos successfully defended their NFL title with a 34-19 victory over the Falcons.

(above)

Neck and Neck

LOUIS NOVICK
NIKON F3

Hialeah Park is listed on the National
Register of Historic Places. In addition to suspenseful finishes and high
stakes, fans enjoy vintage surround-
ings and beautiful grounds.

(opposite)

Nutty

ERNEST PICK
NIKON F4
VELVIA

Found in the names of popular hotels
and shopping districts, the word
"coconut" evokes images of a tropical paradise.

(above)

Any Fish?

ERNEST PICK
NIKON F4
VELVIA

The pelican's plunge is successful
due to its long flattened bill, strong
hook at the tip, and expandable
pouch. Tourists delight in observing
colonies of pelicans near Miami's
shoreline.

(opposite)

Twists and Turns

ERNEST PICK
FUJI, MEDIUM FORMAT
VELVIA, F-16

Massive banyan trees anchor themselves with numerous aerial roots.
Twisted and bundled, banyans
expand to encompass large areas
with the thick canopies.

New and Used

COURTESY OF
GORAN MATIJASEVIC
MINOLTA XE-7
FUJICHROME 100

A furniture shop in Little Havana is
yet another reflection of the presence
of Cuban culture in every aspect of
Miami life.

El Bazar de Coral

COURTESY OF
GORAN MATIJASEVIC
MINOLTA XE-7
FUJICHROME 100

A shop in Little Havana. Although
Miami's Cuban influence is felt in
every aspect of Miami life, Little
Havana is still the Cuban community's vibrant center.

Parqueos

COURTESY OF
GORAN MATIJASEVIC
MINOLTA XE-7
FUJICHROME 100

The arrival of Cuban exiles fleeing
Fidel Castro's regime beginning in
1959 represented a turning point for
Miami, from winter playground to
vibrant, cosmopolitan city. Cuban
immigrants transplanted their artistic, musical and culinary traditions in
south Florida, making it a uniquely,
and fiercely proud Hispanic-
American city.

(top)

Nuestra America

COURTESY OF
GORAN MATIJASEVIC
MINOLTA XE-7
FUJICHROME 100

(bottom)

Cuba

COURTESY OF
GORAN MATIJASEVIC
MINOLTA XE-7
FUJICHROME 100

The Cuban population in Miami is bound together by a singular national and cultural pride. These murals in Little Havana represent the cultural and artistic traditions that Cuban immigrants brought with them, as well as nostalgic longing for their homeland.

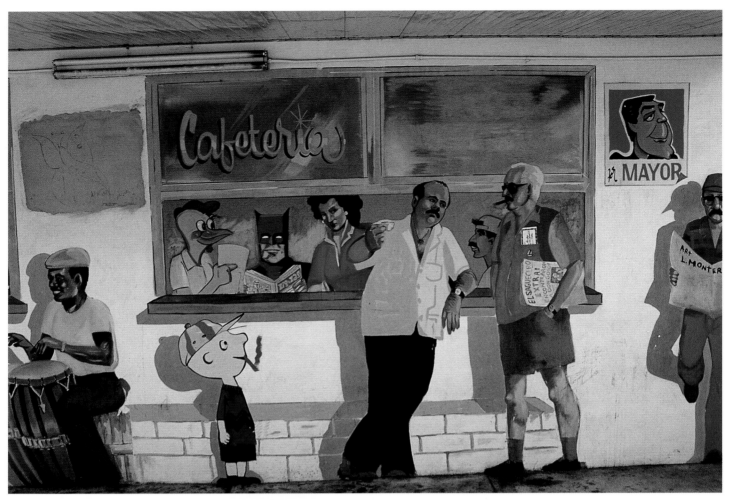

(above)

Cafeteria

COURTESY OF
GORAN MATIJASEVIC
MINOLTA XE-7
FUJICHROME 100

A quirky mural depicts an interesting mix of characters passing time at a Little Havana cafeteria.

(left)

Will She Be Liberty For Me?

HEATHER J. KIRK
OLYMPUS IS-10 SUPER DELUXE
KODAK-64 EKTACHROME, AUTO SETTING

The mural on the exterior of the Haitian Refugee Center in Little Haiti poses the question that penetrates the hearts and minds of many immigrants.

Shade

COURTESY OF
GORAN MATIJASEVIC
MINOLTA XE-7
FUJICHROME 100

Waiting for a bus in Miami requires protection from the elements, rain or shine.

key biscayne

AND BEACHES

(page 36)

Sea Grape Collage

ERNEST PICK
NIKON FY
VELVIA

Hardy sea grape leaves create a dense collage of green.

(above)

Leaves an Impression

ERNEST PICK
NIKON F4
T-MAX 400, F – 5-8

Sunlight and shadow weave an artistic matte of palm leaves.

(opposite)

Moorings

JUDY CASELY

Pleasure craft moored on the calm waters near Key Biscayne await fair weather sailing.

(above)

Picture This!

LAURIE BARKER COE
NIKON N90 S

A trompe l'oeil on the Fontainebleau Hilton Resort and Spa depicts a mirror image of the hotel itself. Grand in scale and history, the Miami Beach hotel has hosted big names in 20th century entertainment like Frank Sinatra.

(left)

Palm and Ocean

HEATHER J. KIRK
OLYMPUS IS-10 SUPER DELUXE
KODAK-64 EKTRACHROME

Steady breezes cool down park- and beach-goers on Key Biscayne. This island paradise is just minutes from downtown Miami, and yet it seems oceans away.

Facade

MICHAEL KELLY
NIKON FM2
FUJI 100, F-8

Palms lit in neon and art deco-styled
palm pillars welcome motorists to
chic Miami Beach. Trendy urban
neighborhoods, stylish boutiques,
and rows of revamped hotels have
created a wonderland referred to as
"SoBe."

(left)
Keeping Watch

HEATHER J. KIRK
OLYMPUS IS-10 SUPER DELUXE
KODAK-64 EKTACHROME

Stark and solid, the Cape Florida Lighthouse has survived both Indian wars and hurricane-force winds.

(opposite)
Shoreline

HEATHER J. KIRK
OLYMPUS IS-10 SUPER DELUXE
KODAK-64 EKTACHROME SLIDE

There is always room for one more chaise or umbrella as tourists and residents head for the pleasures of the sun and surf at Bill Baggs State Recreation Area.

(above)

Captivated

ERNEST PICK
NIKON F4
VELVIA

The great white heron utilizes its S-shaped neck and bill to quickly spear fish in shallow water. Their loose nests can be seen high in the mangroves.

(opposite)

Tropical Color

ERNEST PICK
NIKON F4
VELVIA

A myriad of colors reflects the continuous cycle of growth in a subtropical climate.

Hydro Action

LOUIS NOVICK
NIKON F3

Known for its fast-paced lifestyle, Miami also has speed-driven spectator sports. Hydroplane racing is a popular venue at the Miami Marine Aquarium.

Solitude

LOUIS NOVICK
NIKON F3
EPP

Once a coconut plantation, Crandon
Park offers plenty of R & R. Located
on 1,400 acres, the park provides
some of the best beaches, plenty of
ball fields and picnic areas, as well as
an 18-hole public golf course.

coral gables

AND SOUTH

Tied Up

JUDY CASELEY

Dinner Key Marina is Miami's largest
facility with 575 moorings. The
Coconut Grove Exhibition Center,
adjacent to the marina, hosts a multi-
tude of exhibits and conferences.

Isle Be Away

JUDY CASELEY

Symmetrically balanced, Grove Isle maintains its sense of order and beauty just off the coast of Coconut Grove.

(top)

Renaissance Festival at Villa Vizcaya

COURTESY OF
GORAN MATIJASEVIC
MINOLTA XE-7
FUJICHROME 100

The renaissance-style architecture of Villa Vizcaya serves as an apt backdrop for a renaissance festival's colorful tents.

(bottom)

The Gardens of Vizcaya

COURTESY OF
GORAN MATIJASEVIC
MINOLTA XE-7
FUJICHROME 100

The French and Italian classical gardens that surround Villa Vizcaya barely constrain their opulent tropical growth.

Vizcaya

COURTESY OF
GORAN MATIJASEVIC
MINOLTA XE-7
FUJICHROME 100

Built in 1916 for Michigan industrial-
ist James Deering, Villa Vizcaya was
the creation of three men: F. Burrall
Hoffmann, who designed the buildings, Diego Suarez, who planned
the gardens, and Paul Chalfin, who
acted as the artistic director for the
overall project.

Lawn Games

COURTESY OF
GORAN MATIJASEVIC
MINOLTA XE-7
FUJICHROME 100

An elaborate game of chess is played on the lawn of Vizcaya. Miami-Dade County purchased Vizcaya from Deering's estate in 1952, and after extensive restoration, opened it to the public as a museum. The villa receives almost 200,000 visitors per year, and is host to events ranging from festivals and fundraisers to historic international summits. World leaders and dignitaries, including Presidents, Popes, Kings and Queens have visited Vizcaya.

Pawns

COURTESY OF
GORAN MATIJASEVIC
MINOLTA XE-7
FUJICHROME 100

Living pawns at a renaissance festival
await their orders on the manicured
chessboard at Villa Vizcaya.

(above)

Showtime!

LAURIE BARKER COE
NIKON N90 S

The Coconut Grove Playhouse, which was opened as a cinema in 1926, welcomes touring musicals and European farces.

(opposite)

Tea by the Sea

ERNEST PICK
FUJI, MEDIUM FORMAT
VELVIA, F-16

A stone bridge escorts Vizcaya guests to the Tea House. This unique structure was influenced by French architecture.

(above)

Retreat

LAURIE BARKER COE
NIKON N90S

Spanish and Mediterranean architectural styles are abundant in this quiet haven known as Coral Gables. Entrepreneur and developer George Merrick planned the city during the 1920's land boom.

(left)

Poseidon

ERNEST PICK
FUJI, MEDIUM FORMAT
VELVIA, F-16

Heroes from Greek mythology adorn gardens and fountains throughout Vizcaya. Ten acres of formal gardens provide an enchanting stroll.

(opposite)

Splashy Setting

ERNEST PICK
NIKON F4
T-MAX 400, F-5-8

Poolside diners can admire the architecture and marvel at the enormous swimming pool at the Biltmore Hotel.

(above)

Legal Legacy

JUDY CASELEY
NIKON F4
KODAK 200, F-16

Since the late 1920's, Coral Gables
City Hall has anchored the community with its Spanish-Renaissance style
clock tower and semi-circular design.

(opposite)

Towering Beauty

CARMEN ARROYO
CANON BEBEL
800

Restored in 1993, the Alhambra
Water Tower remains a city landmark.
Its Moorish-style design was com-
pleted originally in 1924.

Dare to Dip?

JUDY CASELEY
NIKON F4
KODAK 200, F-6

Guests at the Biltmore Hotel are
tempted to dip into the inviting
waters of the largest hotel pool in
the United States.

May I?

JUDY CASELEY
NIKON F4
KODAK 200, F-6

Impeccable service and individual-
ized pampering continue to lure
patrons to the Biltmore Hotel in
charming Coral Gables.

Hospitality

JUDY CASELEY

Set amidst the oak-lined streets of Coral Gables, the Biltmore Hotel has become an icon of historical elegance. Grand European traditions reign at this legendary hotel.

(above)

Old-Fashioned Fun

ERNEST PICK
NIKON F4
T-MAX 400, F-5-8

Supplied with spring water daily, the
Venetian Pool basks in the splendor
of waterfalls, coral caves, and
Venetian-style architectural details.

(opposite)

High and Dry

ERNEST PICK
NIKON F4
T-MAX 400, F-5-8

Even when completely drained,
Venetian Pool provides a dramatic
setting. Here, guests enjoy a private
75th birthday celebration.

(above)

Orchid Fall

COURTESY OF
GORAN MATIJASEVIC
MINOLTA XE-7
FUJICHROME 100

Once a typical roadside tourist trap, Miami's Parrot Jungle has evolved into one of South Florida's most lush tropical gardens and animal attractions. This privately owned, 22-acre park is maintained by a dedicated on site horticultural staff which propagate and maintain the gardens' vast tropical plant collection as well as its native landscape.

(left)

White Light

COURTESY OF
GORAN MATIJASEVIC
MINOLTA XE-7
FUJICHROME 100

Parrot Jungle, opened in 1936, began humbly as a trained parrot attraction. The park now exhibits a wide variety of birds and reptiles, including a large collection of exotic parrots, rare tortoises, and other fair fowl.

Ingress

ERNEST PICK

Distressed stone, wood, and metal combine to create a rustic-looking entrance to a private courtyard. Many charming bungalows still exist in this historic area.

Peek!

CYNTHIA CRONIG
MINOLTA 400SI
FUJICHROME, F-11

Watson Island on Biscayne Bay is the
new home of Parrot Jungle, a bird
sanctuary filled with free-flying parrots that love to pose.

Flamingos

COURTESY OF
GORAN MATIJASEVIC
MINOLTA XE-7
FUJICHROME 100

Parrot Jungle, a venerable, 75-year-old tourist tradition, currently occupies one of the last remaining cypress hammocks on the east coast of Florida. Although they are intending to move the attraction to a new location on Watson Island, the owners of this privately-operated park are considering maintaining the original site, with its resident flock of Caribbean flamingos, as a botanical garden.

(above)
Alligator

COURTESY OF
GORAN MATIJASEVIC
MINOLTA XE-7
FUJICHROME 100

In addition to its well-known bird exhibits, Parrot Jungle also exhibits a large collection of native and exotic reptiles, including lizards, rare species of tortoise, and an albino alligator all in naturalistic, non zoo-like settings.

(left)
PrimPing

STANLEY CRONIG
CANON ELAN
FUJICHROME, F-8

Preoccupied with grooming its colorful plumes, this Scarlet Macaw casts a glaring eye.

(above)

Sister Act

COURTESY OF
GORAN MATIJASEVIC
MINOLTA XE-7
FUJICHROME 100

A pair of extravagantly plumed Macaws wow the crowds at Parrot Jungle. Parrot Jungle has come a long way since its days as a roadside attraction, but the park still offers a highly entertaining parrot show. The sight of these magnificent birds doing tricks in costumes or on roller skates, while admittedly goofy, has actually been proven to maintain the mental health and happiness of these highly intelligent, long-lived birds.

(top)

Toucan Play

COURTESY OF
GORAN MATIJASEVIC
MINOLTA XE-7
FUJICHROME 100

A native of Central and South American tropical jungles, a dramatically colored toucan finds itself at home in Miami's Parrot Jungle.

(bottom)

Duets

COURTESY OF
GORAN MATIJASEVIC
MINOLTA XE-7
FUJICHROME 100

A pair of macaws at Parrot Jungle regard the viewer with a worldly eye. *No,* we do not want crackers, thank you. And kindly stop calling us "Polly," *gracias.*

(opposite) Honorable Mention

Nautical Past

RICARDO CRUZ
CANON EOS 1
KODAK GOLD 200, F/22

Nostalgic reminders of a seafaring lifestyle flank many retail businesses and restaurants along the bay.

SOUTH 73 CORAL GABLES AND

(above)

Holiday Palms

JUDY CASELEY
NIKON F4
FUJI 200, F-16

CocoWalk, a three-tiered open-air mall has created a commercial Renaissance in the Grove, which was once a quaint village for writers and artists.

(opposite, top)

Feather Tail

JUDY CASELEY

A powerboat cuts rapidly through calm waters leaving the image of a feather in its wake.

(opposite, top)

Pride

JUDY CASELEY
NIKON F4
KODAK 100, F-6

Opened in 1981, the Miami Metrozoo is dedicated to tropical life with more than 225 species living in natural settings.

Certainly Chinese

ERNEST PICK
FUJI, MEDIUM FORMAT
VELVIA, F-16

Asian influences dominate the architecture in Chinese Village on Riviera
Drive at Menendez Avenue. Villages
sporting an international flair are
scattered throughout Coral Gables.

Go Global

ERNEST PICK
FUJI, MEDIUM FORMAT
VELVIA, F-16

An eclectic mix of architectural styles
creates an international flavor in
Coral Gables. A drive through
Merrick's Villages provides a whirl-
wind tour of over half a dozen global
interpretations.

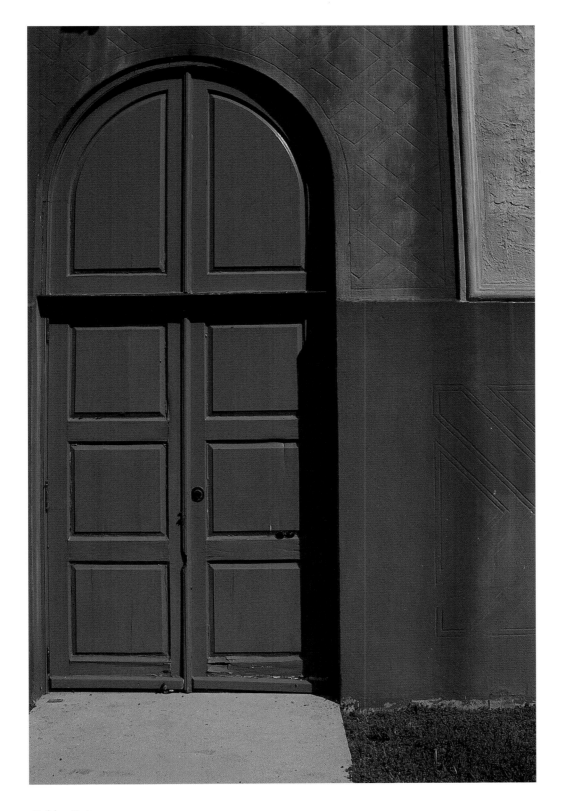

Gables Gate

CATALINA VILLEGAS
NIKON N6006
PROVIA, F/16

The contrasting colors and shapes add interest to the door of the historic Alhambra Water Tower located in Coral Gables.

Unveiling

ERNEST PICK
NIKON F4
VELVIA

Miami's natural beauty is reflected in
the gently curved leaves and dramatic
shadows of its unique vegetation.

Mosaic

JUDY CASELEY
NIKON F4
KODAK 200, F-11

In addition to European influences,
limestone and shells from native
Florida were used to create a regional flair. This intricate ceiling detail is
located in the grotto beneath the
Vizcaya residence.

(opposite)

Talon Time

CYNTHIA CRONIG
MINOLTA 400SI
FUJICHROME, F-16

Distinctive shades of blue and yellow create a contrast of cool and
warm tones on this fanciful macaw.

(above)

Sunset over Miami

COURTESY OF
GORAN MATIJASEVIC
MINOLTA XE-7
FUJICHROME 100

To the west of Miami lies the expanse of the Everglades. Tropical storm clouds that gather over South Florida's vast "River of Grass" create some of the world's most dramatic sunsets

(left)

Groovy Grove Nightlife

COURTESY OF
GORAN MATIJASEVIC
MINOLTA XE-7
FUJICHROME 100

Coconut Grove's groovy, flower-child reputation of the 1960's has been eclipsed in the last few decades by upscale shops, hip cafés and trendy nightclubs.

Evening in the Grove with Sailboats

COURTESY OF
GORAN MATIJASEVIC
MINOLTA XE-7
FUJICHROME 100

Coconut Grove was settled by Bahamian sea merchants in 1834, making it the oldest settlement in South Florida. Because of its convenient proximity to Biscayne Bay, it also came to be considered one of the most important settlements in the region. Now, its unique, hip atmosphere, set apart from nearby downtown Miami, insure that this groovy, tropical village makes it one of the most beloved spots in the country.

south beach

*m*orning, noon, and night, South Beach swings.

Called the new American Riviera, the Two-Mile Jewel, and SoBe, after New York City's fashionable SoHo district, this stretch of broad, white-sand beach, funky, historic, art deco buildings, and delicious tropical weather is home to some of the wildest life on earth.

Nestled on the southern tip of Miami Beach, South Beach is just a stone's throw over the bridge from downtown Miami. But Miami Beach is its own distinct city and South Beach is ground zero for it's own uniquely fabulous cultural fusion. Mambo kings and drag queens; devout Hasidic Jews and self-conscious yuppies; Cuban immigrants, snowbirds, international tourists, celebrities and gawkers alike all add to the rhythm of South Beach's distinctive beat.

South Beach represents one of the largest communities of Art Deco buildings, an architectural style that exemplified the optimism and brilliant decadence of Miami's tourist boom of the 1920's and '30's. Now lovingly restored by dedicated preservationists and savvy entrepreneurs, 800 of South Beach's famous Deco buildings are listed on the National Register of Historic Places. New hotels, celebrity-owned restaurants, chic boutiques, and some of the planet's hippest nightclubs breathe new life into this historic district.

South Beach is also home to a rich arts community. It is the home of the New World Symphony, Ziff Jewish Museum, Bass Museum and the Miami City Ballet as well as numerous other theaters, museums, and art galleries. The Miami Design Preservation League sponsors educational tours, programs and information about the district's architectural history as well as arts festivals and cultural programs.

Sarah FK Coble: Freelance Writer
Sarah FK Coble is a nationally published freelance writer. She is also a contributor to *Florida International Magazine, Naples Illustrated*, and the *Naples Literary Review*. Her work has also been published in the *Sanibel Captiva Review, Gulfshore Life, Gulfshore Style* and *Home and Condo* magazines.

Joe began taking photos of South Beach mornings a year and a half ago. "I've taken thousands of photos of South Beach, primarily at sunrise. It's too bad that most people don't take time out to enjoy the sunrise each day. I hope with my photos, they can see what they're missing," he states. "This photo was taken on Thanksgiving morning and this was truly a morning to be grateful for. The sky was crowded with big, strong clouds." A successful faux finish artist who has resided in South Beach for the past eight years, Joe Johnson also finds creative outlets in photography, painting, and writing.

Sunrise on South Beach, Miami

JOE JOHNSON
CANON EOS
KODAK
AUTO

The golden glow of early morning illuminates Ocean Drive's famous hotel row. Built during Miami's original tourist boom of the 1920's and '30's, South Beach is both a venerable historic district as well as the newest American hot spot.

SECOND PLACE
Dog's Life

JUDY CASELEY
NIKON F4
KODAK 200
F-11

A colorful South Beach resident's pet bichon dog takes a ride down Ocean Drive.

A passionate nature and travel photographer, Judy Caseley also has a keen eye for portraiture as well. Her image of a South Beach man's pampered pet captures the rich diversity and contrast of the faces of South Beach. Currently an elementary school teacher, Judy has been establishing a career in photography and documentary film since the age of 16. Her other award winning photos have appeared in magazines, news publications, museum historical collections, and in books. "Color draws me to a subject," she writes from her home on the rural island of Chokoloskee, Florida. "Bringing a moment to life with color enables me to share the window of treasures that I see." Judy Casely also shot all the aerial photography for *Miami and South Beach: A Photographic Portrait.*

Three Sisters

LIDIA TOHAR
CANON EOS AZE
FUJI, 11

Graceful palm trees are swept by winds off the Atlantic. Situated on the southern tip of the barrier island of Miami Beach, South Beach enjoys the full impact of Atlantic sea breezes and glorious sunsets.

A professional painter and illustrator, Lidia refuses to be confined to a single media. A graduate of Parson's School of Design, this Cuban native expresses her visions not only with canvas and oils, but also with watercolors, ceramics, and photography. "I see myself as an alchemist," she says. "I pick whatever tool is needed, emotionally, at that moment to express my vision and that is where the alchemy begins. These palm trees seemed serene, yet strong, holding themselves up majestically. The day was overcast and windy, but they remained secure in their own space."

(above)

Breakwater, Ocean Drive

COURTESY OF
GORAN MATIJASEVIC
MINOLTA XE-7
FUJICHROME 100

Sharp edges of the streamlined machine like design fantasies of the 1920's are softened by tropical breezes, and palm trees.

(opposite)

China Grill

MICHAEL KELLY
CANON EOS 3
FUJI 100, F5.6

Once a totally cutting edge building in South Beach, with its neo-deco design, the China Grill is now a familiar haunt. Serving healthful, artsy Asian-fusion cuisine this restaurant is still a South Beach favorite among residents, visitors and celebrities.

(above)

South Beach Sales Cart

COURTESY OF
GORAN MATIJASEVIC
MINOLTA XE-7
FUJICHROME 100

Basic, must-have beach souvenirs
and sun protection for sale.

(opposite)

Curious

JUDY CASELEY
MINOLTA 35MM FREEDOM ZOOM 140 EX
KODAK GOLD 200

A flamboyantly coifed South Beach
visitor peeks into the hallway of a
flamboyantly colored apartment
building.

Ocean Drive

COURTESY OF
GORAN MATIJASEVIC
WIDELUX
FUJICHROME 100

Art Deco design was born in Paris in the early 20th century, but south Florida gave the world a whole new perspective on modern style.

Casablanca at the Imperial

COURTESY OF
GORAN MATIJASEVIC
CANON EOS
FUJICHROME 100

After decades of neglect after World
War II, the Imperial Hotel plays
again. With one of the hottest new
Latin American restaurants on
South Beach.

(above)

JUDY CASELEY

This aerial photo shows South Beach with Biscayne Bay and downtown Miami in the distance. The MacArthur and Venetian Causeways connect Miami Beach to Miami. Accessible only by boat a century ago, the bridge from mainland Miami built in 1913 was the catalyst for South Beach's first tourist boom.

(left)

Bon Voyage

WILLIAM WARD MOSELEY
OLYMPUS AZ 230
KODAK 200, 24

South Pointe Park, at the very tip of South Beach, is a good place to view the spectacularly sized cruise ships coming into Port of Miami through Government Cut. Government Cut was dredged in 1905 to provide deep-water passage for Biscayne Bay.

Ocean Discovery

JUDY CASELEY
NIKON F4

Three young beachgoers have made a
discovery on the shore. The broad
Atlantic beaches are the backbone of
South Beach's tropical appeal.

(above)

Guard House at Sunrise

DAVID SOSE
CANON AT-1
VELVIA, F16

The vast, ocean views of the Atlantic are the backbone of South Beach's appeal.

(left)

Sunrise on South Beach

LOUIS NOVICK
NIKON F3
KPL

This is a sight often seen by early risers or all night revelers.

(opposite)

Adrian Hotel and Coconut Palm

LOUIS NOVICK
NIKON F3
FUJI SENSIA

The graceful silhouette of coconut palm fronds swaying in the Atlantic sea breeze animate the façade of the Adrian Hotel.

(above)

Swell

COURTESY OF
GORAN MATIJASEVIC
WIDELUX
FUJICHROME 100

A sweet, cherry convertible and the
Avalon Hotel flaunt their swell curves.

(opposite)

New Deco on the Rise

JUDY CASELEY
NIKON F4
KODAK 200

A newer high rise building on the
southern end of the South Beach
neighborhood reflects Art Deco influence in its design. Just across the
street is the venerable Joe's Stone
Crabs, one of South Beach's most
famous restaurants.

(above)

Red, White, and Blue

BEACH C. EDWARDS
NIKON FM2, 24 MM LENS
FUJI 200

Every visitor to South Beach's sun-soaked shores can find his or her own place in the sun. Many stretches of beach are popular with South Beach's large gay community.

(left)

Riding the Wave

JOHNATHAN ROSE
NIKON F5
KODAK MAX-GOLD 800
17MM, F8.0

Wacky "Wave Mobile" is a rolling advertisement for one of Ocean Drive's boutique hotels and restaurant. Many hotels in Old Miami Beach made themselves more conspicuous through the use of distinctive signage and "Futura" lettering. This car literally gives an old idea a new spin.

Ante Meridian

ABIGAIL POPE
YASHIKA 57 TWINLENS
KODAK PORTRA 160 VC

This romantic, Mediterranean revival style apartment building on Meridian Avenue rises above the bougainvillea to greet the morning light.

(above)

"Tropicool" Cityscape

DAVID SOSE
CANON AT-1
VELVIA, F16

This artful, architectural landscape, taken at Collins Avenue and 15th Street shows South Beach's colorful sense of fun and style.

(opposite)

Makin' Waves

CAROL VERNEUIL
CANON
FUJI VELVIA

A very groovy South Beach lifeguard stand echoes the natural rhythms of the ocean.

Pizza Van

COURTESY OF
GORAN MATIJASEVIC
MINOLTA XE-7
FUJICHROME 100

Soft sand, cool water, warm sun
and hot pizza!

Tail Fins and Racing Stripes

COURTESY OF
GORAN MATIJASEVIC
WIDELUX
FUJICHROME 100

The Colony, with its famous neon
sign and sleek racing stripes, was
one of the best hotels designed by
architect Henry Hohauser.

Hotel Shelley on the Seashore

NANCY J. MEYERS BROWN
CANON EOS REBEL 2000
KODAK MAX 400

Originally built in 1936, the Shelley, a
classic Deco hotel on Collins Avenue
was fully renovated in 1999.

The Berkeley Shores

TIM A. ZELLO
NIKON EM
100, F16

The Berkeley Shores, on Collins Avenue shows classical features of Streamline Moderne design, showing a wide spectrum of influences from sensuous, classical surface decoration, to machine-like elements of science fiction.

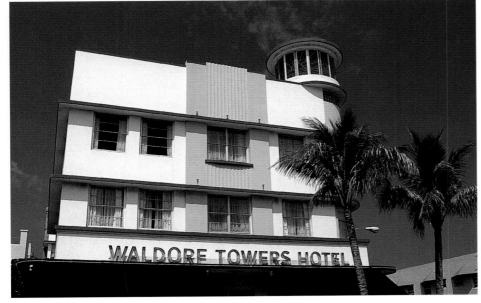

(above)

Hotel Leslie

DAVID SOSE
CANON
VELVIA, F16

The Leslie, built in 1937, shows restrained, sophisticated design, in spite of its cheery, sunny yellow color.

(left)

Waldorf Towers

COURTESY OF
GORAN MATIJASEVIC
MINOLTA XE-7
FUJICHROME 100

The Waldorf's distinctive tower takes its cue from old seaside lighthouses, exemplifying the name, "Nautical Moderne."

(opposite)

Winter Haven

COURTESY OF
GORAN MATIJASEVIC
MINOLTA XE-7
FUJICHROME 100

For all their sleek, chic glamour, the upscale hotels of South Beach are in fact constructed of common, inexpensive building materials. In spite of this, however, the South Beach architects' inventiveness with stucco, terrazzo, lighting and paint became 20th-century design classics.

(above)

Crescent, Ocean Drive

COURTESY OF
GORAN MATIJASEVIC
MINOLTA XE-7
FUJICHROME 100

The gem-like Crescent hotel, sparkles on Ocean Drive. Circles and medallions, taken from ships portholes and Aztec sun symbols were popular applied decoration for sunny Tropical Deco design.

Umbrellas, Tropical Café

COURTESY OF
GORAN MATIJASEVIC
WIDELUX AND MINOLTA XE-7
FUJICHROME 100

Splashily painted umbrellas shade tables in a café in Miami's Caribbean Marketplace serving flavored ice creams and fruit juices.

(above)

Amsterdam Palace

JUDY CASELEY
NIKON F4
KODAK 200

Passers-by stop in line to admire Amsterdam Palace, home of designer Gianni Versace.

(right)

Vigil

DEAN SOLO
OLYMPUS OM4
FUJI RVP, F16

Candles and momentos left on the steps of the Amsterdam Palace, owned by designer Gianni Versace, after the fashion mogul's death.

(above)

Sand Castle

CAROL VERNEUIL
CANON
FUJI VELVIA

This elaborate structure is an ephemeral fantasy in sand. South Beach is often a site for world-class sand-sculpture contests, but many fabulous creations are made for the sheer fun of it.

(above)

Over the Rainbow

LOUIS NOVICK
NIKON F3
EPP

A rainbow after a summer thunderstorm seems to end at the shiny finial of the Marlin Hotel.

Park Central Hotel

DAVID SOSE
CANON
VELVIA, F16

The most famous architect in Miami in 1937, Henry Hohauser, designed this Art Deco masterpiece. The Park Central's style brings the streamlined simplicity of a luxury ocean liner to the shore of Miami Beach.

(above)
McAlpine, Ocean Drive

COURTESY OF
GORAN MATIJASEVIC
MINOLTA XE-7
FUJICHROME 100

The hotels in South Beach's Deco district are typically only 3 to 5 stories tall. Essentially modest in scale, these hotels reflected the machine age optimism that science and technology were the route to progress.

(left)
Parking Spot

COURTESY OF
GORAN MATIJASEVIC
MINOLTA XE-7
FUJICHROME 100

Since finding a good parking spot is always chancy on South Beach, the best way to view the famous district is by foot.

The Clevelander Hotel

COURTESY OF
GORAN MATIJASEVIC
MINOLTA XE-7
FUJICHROME 100

Built in 1938 and designed by architect
Albert Anis, the Clevelander is one of
Ocean Drive's most classic hotels.

(above)

The Carlyle

COURTESY OF
GORAN MATIJASEVIC
MINOLTA XE-7
FUJICHROME 100

Built in 1941, the Carlyle hotel is one of the Deco District's most recent buildings. Its windows show the typical "eyebrow" awnings, which both shaded the windows from the relentless Miami sun, and accentuated the building's streamlined, horizontal lines.

(left)

Bogey

COURTESY OF
GORAN MATIJASEVIC
CANON EOS
FUJICHROME 100

Bogart-era, restored Nash automobile cases the Park Central Hotel.

Holocaust Memorial

MICHAEL KELLY
NIKON FM2
FUJI 100, F11

Kenneth Treister's sobering Holocaust Memorial, completed in 1990, commemorates in bronze and granite the horrific grief of the concentration camps. Miami Beach's Jewish population, still strong even after South Beach's re-gentrification, has one of the largest numbers of Holocaust survivors in the world.

(above)

Lovely Leslie

COURTESY OF
GORAN MATIJASEVIC
CANON EOS
FUJICHROME 100

Built in 1937, the simple elegance
of the diminutive Leslie Hotel
stands as a serene backdrop to
the flamboyant human parade on
Ocean Drive.

(opposite, top)

Adrian and Revere, Ocean Drive

COURTESY OF
GORAN MATIJASEVIC
MINOLTA XE-7
FUJICHROME 100

The Spanish and Mediterranean
influences of the Adrian Hotel's
design, built in 1934, present an
exotic contrast to the sleek lines
and sharp angles of other buildings
in the Deco District.

(opposite, bottom)

Water Tower

COURTESY OF
GORAN MATIJASEVIC
MINOLTA XE-7
FUJICHROME 100

Miami Beach is an island unto itself,
as well as a separate and distinct city
from Metro Miami, across the Bay.

(above)

China Grill–Blue

LOUIS NOVICK
NIKON F3
EPY

This distinctive, multi-level restaurant, designed by New York architect, Jeffrey Beers is now a South Beach landmark. Its exterior sports a sort of retro-deco aesthetic, while its interior is richly appointed with neo-Asian style furnishings and luxurious mosaics, woods, and finishes.

(opposite)

Grill of a Different Color

JUDY CASELEY
NIKON F4
KODAK GOLD 100

China Grill's trademark turret puts on a constantly changing light show for Washington Avenue cruisers.

(above)

The Clevelander by Night

LOUIS NOVICK
NIKON F3
EPY

Neon hues makes South Beach sizzle. A sidewalk table is a great perch for night owls to scope out the nocturnal scene.

(left)

South Beach Tattoo Company

LOUIS NOVICK
NIKON F3
EPY

This establishment on trendy Washington Avenue also caters to South Beach's penchant for edgy fashion statements.

Starlites

MICHAEL KELLY
CANON EOS 3
FUJI 100, F8

When the daylight fades, South
Beach bathes itself in a multicolored
sea of neon lights.

(top)

Twilight Miami

CHRISTIAN C. FROUDE
PENTAX ZX-50
FUJI 100, F16

From a high-rise in South Beach, you can see the bustle and steam of Port of Miami and surrounding islands.

(bottom)

Club Deuce Bar

LOUIS NOVICK
NIKON F3
EPY

Nominated by Miami City Search as "Best Dive Bar," this unassuming joint offers an unpretentious alternative to South Beach's sometimes-unrelenting trendiness. A great jukebox, a not-so-great pool table, cheap, strong drinks, and a late-late night clientele attract a great mix of South Beach's best.

(above)

Edison Lights

MICHAEL KELLY
CANON EOS 3
FUJI 100, F8

Even when the sun goes down, South Beach glows hot.

(right)

Wolf it Down

MICHAEL KELLY
CANON EOS 3
FUJI 200, F-11

The words "plentiful" and "popular" describe Wolfie's famous pastrami sandwiches. This South Beach icon brings forth images of old-fashioned deli dining.

The Sun Also Rises

COURTESY OF
GORAN MATIJASEVIC
CANON EOS
FUJICHROME 100

No one can ever say: "It's just another
sunrise on South Beach." Every sunset
is a spectacularly unique event.

(above)

Casablanca

LAURIE BARKER COE
NIKON N905

South Beach is a dining aficionado's mecca. Casablanca serves up hot Latin American cuisine.

(right)

Strike the Pose

LUCIAN ALEXANDRESCU
F 2.8

A model strikes a pose at a South Beach sushi bar.

Lucian Alexandrescu
1710 Meridian Avenue
Apt. 2
Miami Beach, FL 33139
127

Carmen Arroyo
3921 SW 84 Ave
Miami, FL 34143
51

Judy Casely
PO Box 114
Chokoloskee, FL 34138
*1, 18(2), 39, 50, 51, 60, 62,
63, 64, 74, 75(2), 78, 86, 91,
94, 95, 99, 111, 121*

Laurie Barker Coe
4880 Wecoma Ave
North Port, FL 34287
1, 17, 40, 56, 58, 127

Cynthia Cronig
47 Lakeside Dr East
Centerville, MA 02632
68, 69, 79

Stanley Cronig
47 Lakeside Dr East
Centerville, MA 02632
71

Ricardo Cruz
934 Sorolla Ave
Coral Gables, FL 33134
73

Beach C. Edwards
230 Blue Sky Drive
Durango, CO 81301
100

Christian Froude
37 20th Ave
Venice, CA 90291
124

Joe Johnson
846 Michigan Ave #2
Miami, FL 33139-5641
85

David L. Jones
15465 SW 110th Terrace
Miami, FL 33196
22

Michael Kelly
355 19th St. Apt 206
Miami Beach, FL 33139
41, 89, 117, 123, 125(2)

Heather J. Kirk
5225 E Thomas Rd #109
Phoenix, AZ 85018
18, 34, 40, 42, 43

Goran Matijasevic
420 S. La Esperanza
San Clemente, Ca 92672
*12, 21, 23, 24(2), 2, 30, 31,
32, 33(2), 34, 35, 52(2), 53,
54, 55, 66, 70, 72(2), 90(2),
81, 88, 90, 92, 93, 98, 104,
105, 107, 108, 109, 110(2),
114(2), 115, 116(2), 118,
119(2), 126*

Nancy J. Meyers Brown
4725 Neptune Road
Venice, FL 34293-7836
105

William Ward Mosely
760 Waterford Dr #301
Naples, FL 34113
94

Louis Novick
800 NE 72nd Street
Miami, FL 33138
*6, 7, 8, 13, 14, 16, 20, 25(2),
26, 45, 46, 96, 97, 112, 120,
122(2), 124*

Ernest Pick
4012 Bonita Ave
Coconut Grove, FL 33133
*14, 15, 27, 28, 29, 38, 44,
45, 57, 58, 59, 64, 65, 67,
76(2), 78*

Abigail Pope
1507 Meridian Ave #5
Miami Beach, FL 33139
101

Dr. JohnathanRose
1259 NE 98th Street
Miami Shores, FL 33138
100

Dean Solo
545 NW 1st Avenue
Ft. Lauderdale, Fl 33301
11

David Sose
N. Miami Beach, FL 33160
96, 102, 107, 113

Linda Tohar
2400 Prairie Avenue
Miami, FL 33140
87

Carol Vereuil
33 Woddy Lane
Westport, CT 06880
103,112

Catalina Villlegas
2660 SW 37th Avenue #17
Miami, FL 33133
77

Tim A. Zello
7748 Emerald Cir #201
Naples, FL 34109
106